Spotlight on
ANCIENT CIVILIZATIONS
GREECE

Ancient Greek
DAILY LIFE

Henry Bensinger

Published in 2014 by The Rosen Publishing Group, Inc.
29 East 21st Street, New York, NY 10010

First Edition

Editor: Joanne Randolph
Book Design: Kate Vlachos

Photo Credits: Cover Photos.com/Thinkstock; p. 5 Vladimir Korostyshevskiy/Shutterstock.com; p. 6 Krzysztof Dydynski/Lonely Planet Images/Getty Images; pp. 8, 9, 12, 13, 19 DEA/G. Dagli Orti/De Agostini/Getty Images; pp. 9, 22 DEA/G. Dagli Orti/De Agostini Picture Library/Getty Images; p. 10 DEA Picture Library/De Agostini/Getty Images; p. 11, 18 DEA/A. De Gregorio/De Agostini/Getty Images; pp. 15, 20 DEA/G. Nimatallah/De Agostini Picture Library/Getty Images; p. 16 nevenm/Shutterstock.com; p. 17 Dimitrios/Shutterstock.com; p. 21 General Photographic Agency/Hulton Archive/Getty Images.

Library of Congress Cataloging-in-Publication Data

Bensinger, Henry.
 Ancient Greek daily life / by Henry Bensinger. — First edition.
     pages cm. — (Spotlight on ancient civilizations: Greece)
 Includes index.
 ISBN 978-1-4777-0772-2 (library binding) — ISBN 978-1-4777-0877-4 (pbk.) — ISBN 978-1-4777-0878-1 (6-pack)
 1. Children—Greece—Social life and customs—Juvenile literature. I. Title.
 DF77.B5274 2014
 938—dc23
                                        2013000751

Manufactured in the United States of America

CPSIA Compliance Information: Batch #S13PK2: For Further Information contact Rosen Publishing, New York, New York at 1-800-237-9932

CONTENTS

Family

Ancient Greece was a **civilization** that existed around 2,700 years ago. Their daily lives were much different from our own.

Family was important in ancient Greece, just as it is now, though. Men worked and took part in public meetings. Women were expected to stay at home and care for the children and the household. They would teach their daughters the skills they would need to become wives and run a home, too. Many Greek families owned slaves, who helped with the chores and daily work.

This carving from ancient Greece shows a husband and wife. Once they were married, men and women spent little time together.

Community

Family was important, but the community was important, too. As part of each day the men of the house would go out to work. They worked as farmers, pottery makers, cobblers, fishermen, and officials. Men were also expected to attend community meetings at the **agora**. Here they might vote on issues of the day, crimes, or laws.

At the end of the day, men might gather at the local **gymnasium** to do sports and share the news of the day. In the evening, men might gather at a neighbor's home to share a meal and listen to music as well.

The ancient Greeks built many temples near the agora. Their belief in the many gods and goddesses that controlled all parts of life was one of the things that bound the Greek community together.

The House

Homes in ancient Greece were built to keep people cool in the hot summers and warm in the winters. Most Greek homes had a walled garden or courtyard in the center. The house was built of sun-dried bricks made from mud. Roofs were made of clay tiles.

Ancient Greek homes generally had a storage room to hold grains and containers filled with oil and wine, along with other supplies.

Here a banquet, called a symposium, is being held in the *andron*, or dining room, of a Greek house.

Women generally stayed in the deepest rooms of the house, away from their husbands and any male visitors. Men would entertain male guests in a special room called the **andron**. **Tutors** would use the room during the day to teach lessons to male children.

Marriage

On the morning of the wedding, the bride's feet would be bathed as one of the steps to get her ready for marriage.

All people in ancient Greece were expected to get married. In Athens, girls were married at around age 13. They often married men who were twice their age. In Sparta, men and women married much later in life. They were about the same age as their partners.

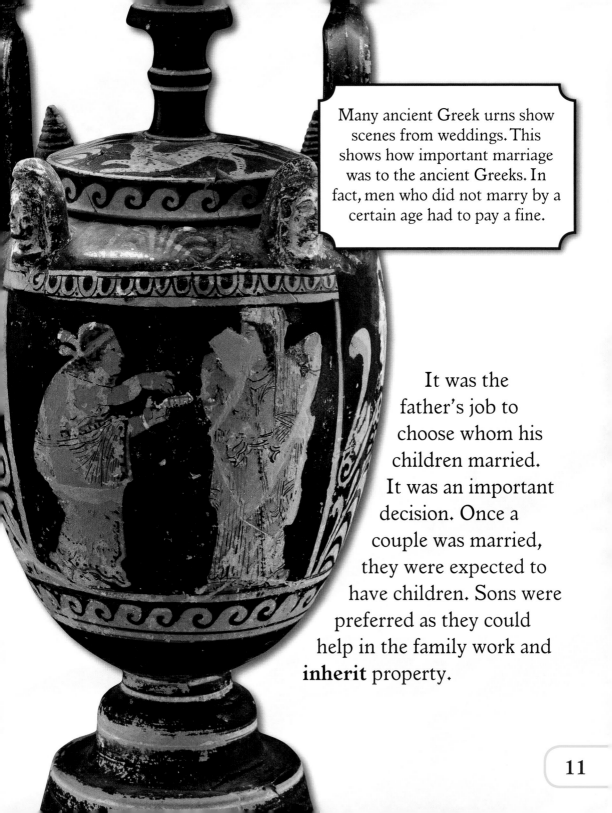

Many ancient Greek urns show scenes from weddings. This shows how important marriage was to the ancient Greeks. In fact, men who did not marry by a certain age had to pay a fine.

It was the father's job to choose whom his children married. It was an important decision. Once a couple was married, they were expected to have children. Sons were preferred as they could help in the family work and **inherit** property.

Women's Role

In wealthy families, women spent much of their time spinning and weaving cloth. They also managed any slaves and kept the household running smoothly. These women rarely went out of the house. If they did go to the market, they never went alone. They went

This carving shows a mother with her daughter. Historians think that ancient Greek mothers and daughters likely had very close relationships.

Greek women spent much of their time weaving and spinning cloth, as this urn from the fifth century BC shows.

with one of their slaves. In poor families, women might work alongside their husbands. They did their own shopping and got water from the town center.

Ancient Greek women were in charge of caring for their children. They taught them the right ways to behave. They taught them the things they would need to run a household, too.

Slavery in Ancient Greece

It was common for Greek families to own slaves. In fact, there were more slaves than there were free citizens in some city-states.

Female slaves worked most often in homes, helping with cooking, cleaning, weaving, and caring for children. Male slaves might work in the **mines**. They might also work at farming or building temples, among other jobs. Slaves worked long hours and had no rights in ancient Greece. It is no wonder that every so often slaves would **revolt**!

Here a young Greek man is shown with one of his slaves.

The Style of the Times

Ancient Greek clothing was generally made from linen or wool fabric. The fabrics were rectangular and fixed with clasps or pins with a belt or sash at the waist. The innermost tunic was a *chiton*. Men wore *chitons*

Here it is easy to see the draped fabric that women of ancient Greece commonly wore.

Men wore clothing made of draped fabric as well, as can be seen on this statue of Plato. Plato was an important Greek thinker and mathematician.

ΠΛΑΤΩΝ

that hung to the knees. Women's *chitons* went to their ankles. A woman might wear a heavier undertunic called a *peplos*. It was held by two clasps at the shoulders.

Greek men sometimes wore a kind of cloak that was made from a loop of fabric. In winter a longer, heavier cloak was worn. It was called a *himation*.

Mealtimes in Ancient Greece

These clay copies of fruit and cheese, common foods eaten in ancient Greece, were buried in an ancient Greek tomb.

Most ancient Greeks worked as farmers. They grew grains such as barley and wheat. They also grew olives and grapes. Women ground the grains into flour for bread or made porridge. The olives were pressed for their oil. Grapes were used to make wine.

Many Greeks also raised goats or other animals. Milk from these animals could be used to make cheese. Lentils, peas, beans, apples, and other foods were also part of their diet.

Because many Greek city-states were on the coast, fish and shellfish were also staples of their diet.

Men often held banquets, or symposia, each night. Other male guests came to eat and drink wine, while musicians entertained them.

Childhood

Ancient Greek children were known to play with some of the same toys as children today do. Remains of ancient dolls, yo-yos, hoops, and balls have been found in Greece. It was not all fun and games for Greek children, though.

This statue from the second century BC shows a young Greek boy riding a horse.

This image was copied from a piece of ancient Greek pottery. It shows a child playing with a yo-yo.

Greek boys began to attend school around the age of seven. They learned history, reading, writing, and math. They also learned music and poetry. They spent time each day practicing athletics and learning to be soldiers. Girls stayed at home and learned weaving, cooking, and other skills needed to run a household.

Sports and Entertainment

Fitness was an important part of daily Greek life. Boys and men spent time each day doing sports, such as running, wrestling, and throwing the **javelin** or **discus**.

The Greeks liked other forms of entertainment as well. Citizens enjoyed going to the theater. At **banquets**, musicians and dancers were hired to entertain guests. Studying the daily lives of the ancient Greeks can tell us a lot about this important civilization.

People would come to watch athletes compete in events, such as running, riding, chariot racing, and more. Chariots, such as the one shown in this carving, were also used in wars.

GLOSSARY

agora (A-guh-ruh) A market in ancient Greece.

andron (AN-dron) A room, filled with couches, cushions, and oil lamps, in which men had guests and parties called symposia.

banquets (BAN-kwets) Large meals eaten in honor of holidays or special events.

chiton (KY-ton) A sewn tunic, or long shirt without sleeves.

civilization (sih-vih-lih-ZAY-shun) People living in a certain way.

discus (DIS-kis) A cirluclar disk that is thrown.

gymnasium (jim-NAY-zee-um) A sports center.

inherit (in-HER-it) To receive something from a parent.

javelin (JAV-uh-lin) A light spear used as a weapon or thrown in a competitive sport.

mines (MYNZ) Pits or underground tunnels from which stones are taken.

revolt (rih-VOLT) To fight or rebel.

tutors (TOO-terz) People who teach one student or a small group of students.

INDEX

WEBSITES

Due to the changing nature of Internet links, PowerKids Press has developed an online list of websites related to the subject of this book. This site is updated regularly. Please use this link to access the list:
www.powerkidslinks.com/sacg/life/